S0-AJS-844

LONDON

LONDRES

A Book of Photographs by
R. S. MAGOWAN

With an Introduction by
A. P. HERBERT

SPRING BOOKS · LONDON

Published by

SPRING BOOKS

WESTBOOK HOUSE • FULHAM BROADWAY • LONDON

© Paul Hamlyn Ltd., 1959

First published 1959
Revised reprint, 1960
Second Impression 1963

T 1115

Printed in Czechoslovakia

Contents

THE ARMS OF THE CITY OF LONDON
LES ARMES DE LA CITÉ DE LONDRES
WAPPEN DER CITY LONDON

Introduction

WE all love London. Even Americans, fresh from the electric city of New York, love London. But how little most of us know of it! I should know more than most. As a boy I lived in Kensington; as an undergraduate I spent a lot of time in the East End at the Oxford House Settlement; and I was married in the Red Church in Bethnal Green Road. For forty years I have lived at the other end, at Hammersmith. All through the last war I was in and out of Dockland, and I have made, I suppose, a thousand voyages from end to end of London — by the river. I have marched in a Lord Mayor's Procession, climbed the Monument and Big Ben's Tower, and seen the new-crowned Queen go by from New Palace Yard. These beautiful photographs are full of memories: but they remind me too how much I have still to learn.

I love London for a thousand reasons: for its simple people, for its elaborate pomp and pageantry, for its pubs and palaces, for its parks and public shows, for its elegant old buildings and charming quiet corners where you might be in a village a hundred miles away—Chelsea, Highgate, Hammersmith—for its variety, its planless splendours, its untidy twists and turns, for its massive order and efficiency, for its police, its postmen, its taximen and busmen, for all the thousands who serve us, on the whole, with a will and a smile; for its sudden changes of scene and climate, as when you pass from the City into Aldgate East, or steaming up the river by night come through Blackfriars Bridge from the gloom of deserted wharves and warehouses to the blaze and bustle of the Embankment, Waterloo Bridge and the lights of Parliament.

The people—the simple, solid, gay, courageous people. I began to get to know them in those far days in Whitechapel and Bethnal Green. One of my jobs was to go from house to house, in summer, in the hot unlovely streets, making arrangements for that splendid institution, the Children's Country Holiday Fund. Afterwards I used to help escort the long crocodile of hilarious and labelled children—80 to 100 of them—from Bethnal Green to Euston or Waterloo, an anxious journey by Underground. I remember the alarming scene when 70 small children rushed on to a moving staircase ahead of their escorts and piled up at the top in a yelling heap. I learned a lot about the people then. I shall never forget the sights and sounds of the Bethnal Green Road, the costers' flares and caustic merry banter, that noble highway, the Whitechapel High Street, the well-dressed walkers on Saturday night.

My river roamings took me back to those fascinating regions, to Rotherhithe, to Wapping and Blackwall, to the men who work on the water or beside it. I know Bow Creek and Barking Creek and have been through the Limehouse Cut. I once knew every waterside pub from Southwark to Southend, including many, alas, that have been done to death by the war or the Licensing Justices.

And so I love the pubs, for there (forget for a moment about 'drinks' and 'alcohol') you can meet the people on equal terms: it is the nearest thing in any country to a 'classless society'. I took Mr Menzies, Prime Minister of Australia, to my 'local' and proudly said, 'You have nothing like this, sir.' 'No, indeed,' he said, 'nor has anyone else.'

London is, without doubt, physically a mess—'The great wen', Cobbett said; but what a glorious wen! It is twenty miles by river from my home to the Woolwich Free Ferry—fifteen miles, I suppose, by crow. Yet both come under the London County Council. How absurd! But in that twenty miles what a rich variety of history and present life the lightermen and tugmen see! Sailing races at Hammersmith and Putney, rowing-boats as busy as water-beetles in the summer and in the winter that multitude of water-birds, sheltering from storm: the herring-gull, the black-head and the black-back, the cormorant and the coot, the heron and the tufted duck. The birds, at least, know that London is on the sea. And have I not seen a porpoise in Chelsea Reach and a seal on Chiswick Eyot? We have the blackbird too, and, long ago, I saw a kingfisher fly past my garden. It was four o'clock in the morning, true, and I was in evening dress—but I did.

Wandsworth—Fulham—half a mile from the haunts of birds and boats—but there are great colliers unloading coal from Newcastle. Those mighty power stations, one after another! Are we in some industrial city of the North? No, no, here is Chelsea, the Capital of Art, with gracious little houses, and delicious corners of tranquillity. Opposite, a great park—and, of all things, a Fun Fair! Round the corner, a first glimpse of St Paul's. Then suddenly Westminster in all its glory—Cleopatra's Needle—the Savoy—Waterloo Bridge—The Temple—Captain Scott's ship and the Master Mariners and the Navy. Variety—and seagulls still.

Then through Blackfriars Bridge into another world—the worst muddle in London—Wren's Cathedral fighting to be seen behind dingy warehouses and a criminal telephone exchange—another power house opposite—and what do you think?—a cluster of *swans*, placid in the filthy water, or paddling in the mud. A crazy scene. And Shakespeare's theatre was just behind that warehouse.

London Bridge, and three fine buildings that we do not conceal—Fishmongers Hall, the Customs House and the Tower. Tower Bridge, unique, odd, but excellent. And still we have ten miles to go for Woolwich Arsenal—ten miles of docks and wharves and shipping, ten miles of the greatest Port in the world. Not beautiful miles—not like the Seine; but halfway there is one more of those mad surprises, the Palace of Greenwich gleaming like a jewel in a dust-bin—and behind it, by the way, the National Maritime Museum, about the best thing in London.

I love London for its massive efficiency. Think of it—eight million souls and more, as many as the entire population of Australia, huddled together in a few square miles round Westminster—to say nothing of the millions more who travel in and out each day from Greater London! Think of the business of feeding, watering, warming, lighting, housing, transporting, entertaining such a multitude in such a space. The power stations dotted along the Thames from Kingston to Blackwall—the colliers ploughing down the North Sea and up through the bridges to supply them—the Thames Valley and all its distant streams working away to give you water—the dust-bins and waste-paper baskets and drains of the Great Wen—the tangle of tubes and tunnels and pipes and sewers and conduits and cables in the bowels of London, as sensitive and complex as the inside of a man. Every time a Londoner turns a tap, presses a switch, boils an egg, uses bin or bathroom, telephones or travels, he should say to himself, 'This is a miracle.' One would say that if you touched so delicate a web at any point, the whole must collapse. But, as we saw in the last war, in good and loyal hands, it has a magical solidity.

Most, no doubt, I love the river: and that is no mere personal peculiarity. Without the river there would have been no London—and London could not live today. It is your larder, your cistern, your light and heat—your history. You should love the river too.

In this fine picture-gallery, London by land, of course, prevails: but here, as well, is the richness of London River—the stately Tower Bridge in action, the ancient Tower (which somehow manages to look like a new toy always), and below it, the Cockney children playing in the sand (Did you know that, on the inspiration of that great Londoner, 'Tubby' Clayton, all that sand was lovingly brought by water in 1934 to make an East End *plage*?); St Paul's; that noble view from Blackfriars Bridge with the gay little summer clouds; loaded lighters waiting on the buoys; Somerset House in floodlight, Parliament, and the Clock Tower, the Sphinx, the County Hall, the dockyard cat, the Tate—and the statue of Samuel Plimsoll that few of you have seen.

If you have never wandered about London with a questing, noticing eye before, you will now.

6

Introduction

NOUS aimons tous Londres. Même les Américains, venant de cette ville électrisante qu'est New-York, aiment Londres. Mais comme nous la connaissons mal, pour la plupart! Je devrais la connaître mieux que beaucoup. Enfant, j'habitais Kensington; étudiant à l'université, je passais beaucoup de temps dans l'East End, à l'Oxford House Settlement; et je me suis marié à Red Church, dans Bethnal Green Road. Depuis quarante ans, maintenant, j'habite Hammersmith, à l'autre bout de Londres. Pendant toute la dernière guerre, j'ai passé mon temps à aller et venir entre mon domicile et les docks, et je pense que j'ai dû faire mille trajets d'un bout à l'autre de Londres — sur le fleuve. J'ai fait partie du cortège du Lord Mayor, je suis monté en haut du Monument et de la tour de Big Ben, et j'ai vu de New Palace Yard passer la Reine au retour de son couronnement. Ces belles photographies sont pour moi riches de souvenirs ; mais elles me rappellent, aussi, combien j'ai encore à apprendre.

J'aime Londres pour mille raisons ; pour ses habitants qui sont simples, pour son faste et l'apparat de ses cérémonies, pour ses « pubs » et ses palais, ses parcs et ses spectacles publics, ses élégantes maisons anciennes et ses charmants coins tranquilles, Chelsea, Highgate, Hammersmith, où l'on se croirait dans un village à plus de cent cinquante kilomètres de la capitale ; pour la variété qu'on y trouve, pour sa splendeur disparate, ses rues enchevêtrées, la solidité de son ordre et son efficacité, pour son corps de police, ses facteurs, ses chauffeurs de taxis et ses employés d'autobus, pour la foule de ceux qui nous y servent, avec bonne grâce, pour la plupart ; pour ses changements subits d'aspect et de climat, comme lorsqu'on passe de la City à Aldgate East, ou bien quand à la nuit on remonte le fleuve et que, laissant derrière soi les ténèbres désertes des quais et des entrepôts de marchandises, on dépasse Blackfriars Bridge pour se retrouver au milieu des lumières et de l'animation de l'Embankment, de Waterloo Bridge et du Parlement.

Les habitants — ces gens simples, solides, gais et courageux, j'ai commencé à les connaître au temps lointain de mes visites à Whitechapel et à Bethnal Green. Une des tâches que j'avais à remplir, me conduisait de maison en maison, le long de rues sans attrait, dans la chaleur accablante de l'été, pour le compte de cette merveilleuse institution qu'est le « Children's Country Holiday Fund ». Ensuite, j'accompagnais une longue rangée d'enfants joyeux et étiquetés — 80 ou 100 d'entre eux — qui se rendaient de Bethnal Green à la gare d'Euston ou de Waterloo, trajet inquiétant qui se faisait par métro. Je me souviens du jour où quelque 70 enfants, abandonnant leurs moniteurs, se précipitèrent dans l'escalier roulant, et s'entassèrent en un bruyant amoncellement au faîte de l'escalier. En ce temps-là, j'appris à connaître le peuple. Je n'oublierai jamais le spectacle ni les bruits de Bethnal Green Road, les lampes à huile des marchands des quatre saisons et leurs plaisanteries caustiques; cette grand'rue qu'est Whitechapel High Street ; les promeneurs bien habillés du samedi soir.

Mes vagabondages sur la Tamise me ramenèrent en ces endroits extraordinaires : Rotherhithe, Wapping, Blackwall, à ces hommes qui travaillent sur l'eau ou sur les rives. Je connais Bow Creek et Barking Creek, et j'ai passé le Limehouse Cut. Il fut une époque où je connaissais tous les « pubs » du bord de l'eau depuis Southwark jusqu'à Southend, y compris beaucoup de ceux qui ont été condamnés, hélas, soit par la guerre soit par les « licensing justices ».

Oui, j'aime les « pubs », car c'est là (oublions pour l'instant les « apéritifs » et « l'alcool ») que les inégalités sociales s'effacent les mieux : le « pub » est ce qui se rapproche le plus, où que ce soit, d'une société sans classe. J'ai emmené M. Menzies, Premier Ministre d'Australie, au « pub » de mon quartier, et je lui ai dit avec fierté : « Vous n'avez rien de pareil dans votre pays, Monsieur. » « Cela est bien vrai, » m'a-t-il répondu ; « ni personne dans aucun autre pays.»

Londres est, sans aucun doute, un fouillis du point de vue morphologique. « La grande verrue », ainsi que Cobbett l'a appelée : mais quelle belle verrue ! Il y a trente kilomètres, environ, en suivant le fleuve, entre mon domicile et le Woolwich Free Ferry — vingt-deux kilomètres, je suppose, à vol d'oiseau. Tous deux, pourtant, sont du ressort du London County Council. C'est absurde ! Mais quelle richesse d'histoire, quelle variété d'aspects peuvent observer sur ce parcours de trente kilomètres, les mariniers et les pilotes ! L'été, des régates à Hammer-smith et à Putney, des canots aussi animés que des dytiques et, en hiver, la multitude d'oiseaux aquatiques qui s'abritent contre le tempête : la mouette argentée, la noire, le cormoran ou la foulque, le héron ou le canard à houppe. Les oiseaux, du moins, savent que Londres donne sur la mer. Et ne m'est-il pas arrivé de voir un mar-souin à Chelsea Reach et un phoque à Chiswick Eyot? Les merles, aussi, nous rendent visite, et j'ai vu, il y a long-temps déjà, un martin-pêcheur survoler mon jardin. C'était à quatre heures du matin, et j'étais en tenue de soirée — mais je l'ai vraiment vu.

Wandsworth — Fulham à moins d'un kilomètre des cotres et des oiseaux, voici de grands charbonniers déchargeant le charbon de Newcastle. Voici, l'une après l'autre, ces puissantes centrales électriques. Sommes-nous dans quelque ville industrielle du nord? Non, nous sommes bien à Chelsea, la capitale des beaux-arts de Londres, avec d'élégantes petites maisons et de délicieux coins tranquilles. En face, se trouvent un parc et, de toutes choses-une foire! C'est non loin de là — qu'on aperçoit pour la première fois la Cathédrale St-Paul. Puis soudain West-minster dans toute sa gloire — l'Aiguille de Cléopâtre — le Savoy Hotel — Waterloo Bridge — le Temple — le bateau du capitaine Scott, et les Master Mariners et la Marine. Que de variété ! — et voici encore des mouettes.

On passe ensuite sous Blackfriars Bridge pour arriver dans un autre monde — le pire désordre de tout Londres — la cathédrale de Wren, cachée derrière de crasseaux entrepôts et un lamentable bâtiment de l'admi-nistration des P. T. T. — en face, une autre centrale électrique et — l'on à peine en croire ses yeux — un groupe de cygnes, voguant placidement sur cette eau dégoûtante, ou bien barbotant dans la vase. Spectacle inimaginable! Quand on pense que le théâtre de Shakespeare se trouvait juste derrière un de ces entrepôts!

Suivent ensuite London Bridge et trois beaux édifices que nous n'essayons pas de cacher — Fishmongers Hall, la Douane, et la Tour de Londres. Tower Bridge, qui est unique, bizarre, mais très réussi. Puis il y a une quinzaine de kilomètres à parcourir avant d'atteindre l'arsenal de Woolwich — quinze kilomètres de docks, de quais et de navires, quinze kilomètres du plus grand port du monde. Ce n'est pas bien sûr, une avenue royale — ce n'est pas la Seine ; mais, à mi-chemin, voici encore une de ces surprises insensées, le Palais de Greenwich, qui brille comme un joyau au fond d'une poubelle et, derrière lui, soit dit en passant, le Musée Maritime National, qui est à peu près ce qu'il y a de mieux à Londres.

J'aime Londres pour sa solide efficacité. Songez-y : huit millions d'âmes au moins, autant que la population de toute l'Australie, se coudoient sur quelques kilomètres carrés autour de Westminster — sans compter les mil-lions qui, chaque jour, font l'aller et retour entre la ville et la banlieue éloignée — le « grand Londres ». Songez à ce que représentent la ravitaillement, l'approvisionnement en eau et en électricité, le chauffage, le logement, le transport et les loisirs d'une telle fourmilière ! Ces centrales réparties le long de la Tamise de Kingston à Black-wall — ces charbonniers qui sillonnent la Mer du Nord et remontent le fleuve pour venir les alimenter — cette vallée de la Tamise et tous ses cours d'eau éloignés qui nous approvisionnent en eau — ces poubelles et ces cor-beilles et ces égouts de la Grande Verrue — cet enchevêtrement de tubes, de tunnels, de tuyaux, de conduits souterrains et de câbles qui foisonnent dans les entrailles de Londres, aussi sensibles, aussi complexes que celles de l'homme ! Chaque fois qu'un Londonien ouvre un robinet, qu'il appuie sur un bouton, qu'il fait cuire un œuf à la coque, qu'il se sert de la poubelle, de la salle de bains ou du téléphone, ou qu'il entreprend un voyage, il devrait se dire : « Ceci est un miracle. » Car il semble qu'au moindre contact ce réseau si délicat va s'effouvrer. Pourtant en de bonnes et fidèles mains, l'édifice est doué d'une solidité magique, ainsi que nous l'avons constaté pendant la dernière guerre.

Plus que tout, sans doute, j'aime le fleuve : et ceci n'est pas une singularité personnelle. Sans la Tamise, Londres n'eût jamais existé — et Londres ne pourrait pas vivre aujourd'hui. La Tamise est le garde-manger de Londres, sa citerne, sa lumière et son foyer — son histoire. Vous pouvez l'aimer vous aussi.

C'est naturellement la ville, et non le fleuve, qui tient la première place dans le joli recueil que voici : mais on y voit aussi toute la richesse du fleuve de Londres — le majestueux Tower Bridge en mouvement, la vieille Tour de Londres (qui parvient toujours à ressembler à un jouet nouveau) et, sous ses murs, les enfants cockneys qui jouent dans le sable (savez-vous que, sur l'initiative de ce grand Londonien, « Tubby » Clayton, tout ce sable fut débarqué avec amour, en 1934, afin que les habitants de l'East End aient une plage?) ; la Cathédrale St-Paul ; le noble perspective qu'on aperçoit de Blackfriars Bridge, avec ces gais petits nuages d'été ; des chalands tout chargés, amarrés aux bouées ; Somerset House illuminé, le Parlement, et la Tour de l'Horloge, le Sphinx, le County Hall, le chat de chantier, la Tate Gallery — et la statue de Samuel Plimsoll que peu de Londoniens ont vue.

Si vous n'avez jamais erré dans Londres en enquêteur ou en observateur, vous le ferez désormais.

THE ARMS OF THE LONDON COUNTY COUNCIL
LES ARMES DU CONSEIL DU COMTÉ DE LONDRES
WAPPEN DES LONDONER GRAFSCHAFTSRATS

Einleitung

WER liebte London nicht? Sogar Amerikaner, die frisch aus der elektrisierenden Stadt New York kommen, lieben es. Aber wie wenig wissen die meisten von uns über London! Ich selbst müßte es eigentlich besser kennen. Als Junge lebte ich in Kensington; als Student verbrachte ich einen Großteil meiner Zeit im Ostend beim Oxford House Settlement; und ich wurde in der Red Church in Bethnal Green Road getraut. Vierzig Jahre lang wohnte ich am anderen Ende der Stadt, in Hammersmith. Während des ganzen letzten Krieges ging ich im Hafengebiet aus und ein, und ich schätze, ich habe an die tausend Fahrten vom einen Ende Londons zum andern hinter mir — immer auf dem Fluß. Ich bin im Zug des Lord Mayor marschiert, bin auf das Monument und den Big Ben geklettert und habe die neu gekrönte Königin vom New Palace Yard vorbeiziehen sehen. Diese herrlichen Photographien sind für mich voll von Erinnerungen; aber sie gemahnen mich auch daran, wie viel ich noch zu lernen habe.

Ich liebe London aus tausenderlei Gründen: wegen seiner einfachen Menschen, wegen seines vollendeten Prunks und seines Glanzes, wegen seiner Schenken und Paläste, wegen seiner Parks und öffentlichen Vergnügungen, wegen seiner eleganten alten Bauten und seiner reizenden verschwiegenen Winkel, in denen man sich vorkommt wie in einem Dorf hundertfünfzig Kilometer weiter — Chelsea, Highgate, Hammersmith —, wegen seiner Vielfalt, seiner regellosen Pracht, seiner unübersichtlichen Ecken und Windungen, wegen seiner festgefügten Ordnung und Tüchtigkeit, seiner Polizei, seiner Postbeamten, seiner Taxi- und Autobusfahrer, wegen all der Tausende, die uns, im großen und ganzen, rasch entschlossen und mit freundlichem Lächeln zu Diensten stehen; und schließlich liebe ich es wegen seiner plötzlichen Wechsel in der Szenerie und im Charakter, — wenn man zum Beispiel von der Innenstadt nach Aldgate East kommt oder wenn man auf einer nächtlichen Dampferfahrt flußaufwärts unter Blackfriars Bridge hindurch aus dem Dunkel verlassener Ankerstellen und Lagerhallen in das flimmernde und geschäftige Treiben des Kais und der Waterloo Bridge und den Lichterglanz der Parlamentsgebäude gerät.

Und dann das Volk — die einfachen, echten, fröhlichen, tapferen Menschen. Ich begann sie kennenzulernen in jenen fernen Tagen in Whitechapel und Bethnal Green. Eine meiner Beschäftigungen bestand darin, im Sommer die heißen, reizlosen Straßen entlang von Haus zu Haus zu gehen und für die hervorragende Einrichtung des Children's Country Holiday Fund (Fonds zur Finanzierung von Kinder-Landaufenthalten) zu werben. Später half ich gewöhnlich dabei, die lange Schlange springlebendiger und mit Namensschildern versehener Kinder — jeweils 80 bis 100 — von Bethnal Green zur Euston- oder Waterloo-Station zu bringen — eine schwierige und unruhige Reise mit der Untergrundbahn. Ich erinnere mich an die aufregende Szene, als 70 kleine Kinder ihren Begleitern voran auf eine Rolltreppe zustürzten und sich am oberen Ende zu einem quietschenden und tosenden Haufen zusammenballten! Damals lernte ich so manches über die Menschen dort. Niemals werde ich die Bilder und Klänge der Bethnal Green Road vergessen, die fliegenden Händler, die mit Geschrei und derb-fröhlichen Witzen ihre Waren anpriesen, die vornehme Prachtstraße, die Whitechapel High Street, und die gutgekleideten Spaziergänger am Samstag abend.

Meine Streifzüge auf dem Fluß brachten mich zurück zu den fesselnd interessanten Gebieten von Rotherhithe, Wapping und Blackwall, zu den Männern, die auf dem Wasser oder am Rand des Wassers arbeiten. Ich kenne Bow Creek, Barking Creek und sogar den Limehouse Cut. Ich kannte einst jede Hafenschenke von Southwark bis Southend, einschließlich so mancher, die ein Opfer des Krieges oder der Konzessionsbehörden wurde. Ich liebe diese Schenken, denn dort (vergessen wir einen Moment das Trinken und den Alkohol) sieht man sich den Menschen aus dem Volk als Gleicher unter Gleichen gegenüber: ein Zustand, der von allem Vergleichbaren in den verschiedenen Ländern der Erde der „klassenlosen Gesellschaft" am nächsten kommt. Ich nahm eines Tages den australischen Ministerpräsidenten Menzies in mein „Stammlokal" und erklärte stolz: „Das gibt es bei Ihnen nicht." — „Nein, wirklich nicht", erwiderte er, „und auch nirgends sonst."

London ist, äußerlich gesehen, zweifellos eine ungestalte Masse — eine „Riesengeschwulst". (Cobbett meinte dazu: „Aber was für eine herrliche Geschwulst!") Von meiner Wohnung bis Woolwich Free Ferry sind es auf dem Fluß dreißig Kilometer — Luftlinie, schätze ich, zweiundzwanzig Kilometer. Und beide unterstehen — unvorstellbar genug — dem Londoner Grafschaftsrat! Aber welche Vielfalt an Geschichte und Gegenwart bekommen auf diesen dreißig Kilometern die Männer auf den Leichtern und Schleppern zu sehen! Wettsegeln auf der Höhe von Hammersmith und Putney, im Sommer Ruderboote, die geschäftig wie die Wasserkäfer hin- und herflitzen, im Winter die Vielzahl der Wasservögel, die vor dem Sturm Schutz suchen: Heringsmöwe, Seeschwalbe und Mantelmöwe, Kormoran und Bläßhuhn, Reiher und Reiherente. Wenigstens die Vögel wissen, daß London an der See liegt. Und habe ich nicht in Chelsea Reach einen Tümmler und auf Chiswick Eyot eine Robbe gesehen? Auch Schwarzdrosseln gibt es bei uns, und vor langer Zeit sah ich hinter meinem Garten einen Eisvogel vorbeifliegen. Zugegeben: es war vier Uhr morgens, und ich war im Abendanzug, — aber ich habe ihn gesehen!

In Wandsworth und Fulham — nur einen Kilometer von den Schlupfwinkeln der Vögel und der Kähne entfernt — löschen große Kohlenschiffe das schwarze Gold aus Newcastle. Eins ums andere reihen sich dort die gewaltigen Kraftwerke aneinander. Sehen wir uns plötzlich in einer Industriestadt des Nordens? Aber nein, wir sind in Chelsea, dem Zentrum der Kunst, mit seinen anmutigen kleinen Häusern und entzückenden verschwiegenen Winkeln. Auf der anderen Seite ein riesiger Park und vor allen Dingen — ein Rummelplatz! Ein Blick um die Ecke — da taucht zum erstenmal St. Paul's Cathedral auf. Und dann liegt plötzlich Westminster in all seinem Glanz vor uns — die Nadel der Cleopatra — das Savoy — Waterloo Bridge — The Temple — Kapitän Scotts Schiff „Discovery", die Master Mariners und die Navy. Welch ein Reichtum! — und noch immer Seemöwen.

Dann kommen wir unter Blackfriars Bridge hindurch in eine andere Welt, das schlimmste Durcheinander in ganz London. Wren's Cathedral verschwindet fast hinter düsteren Lagerhallen und einem geradezu unerlaubten Fernsprechamt, gegenüber liegt wieder ein Kraftwerk, und inmitten all dessen — was meint man wohl? — eine Gruppe von *Schwänen*, die majestätisch auf dem schmutzigen Wasser ruhen oder im Schlamm herumpaddeln. Ein paradoxes Bild! Und ausgerechnet hinter diesen Hallen lag Shakespeares Theater.

Weiter zur London Bridge und drei schönen Gebäuden, über die wir nicht hinweggehen wollen: Fishmongers Hall, Customs House und der Tower. Die Tower Bridge — einzigartig, merkwürdig, aber hervorragend. Und immer noch sind es fünfzehn Kilometer bis zum Woolwich Arsenal — fünfzehn Kilometer lang nur Docks und Kais und Schiffe, fünfzehn Kilometer lang der größte Hafen der Welt. Es sind keine schönen fünfzehn Kilometer, nicht vergleichbar mit der Seine; doch auf halber Strecke liegt wieder eine jener Überraschungen, die aller Vernunft Hohn sprechen: der Palace of Greenwich, gleichsam ein leuchtendes Juwel in einem Kehrichteimer, — dahinter übrigens das National Maritime Museum, so ziemlich die beste Einrichtung Londons.

Ich liebe London wegen seiner geballten Geschäftigkeit. Man stelle sich das vor: acht Millionen Menschen und mehr, so viel wie die ganze Bevölkerung von Australien, zusammengedrängt auf einige wenige Quadratkilometer rund um Westminster, — ganz zu schweigen von den Millionen Pendlern, die jeden Tag aus Groß-London hereinkommen! Man braucht nur an die Aufgabe zu denken, eine solche Menge auf so engem Raum mit

Nahrung, Wasser, Wärme, Licht, Wohnraum, Transportmitteln und Unterhaltung zu versorgen! An die Kraftwerke, die von Kingston bis Blackwall über das Themseufer verstreut sind — die Kohlenschiffe, die in südlicher Richtung die Nordsee durchpflügen und unter Brücken hindurch die Themse hinauffahren, um die Kraftwerke zu versorgen — das Themsetal und all seine entfernteren Zuflüsse, die sich gemeinsam bemühen, der Bevölkerung Wasser zu bringen — die Abfalleimer und Papierkörbe und Gullys der Riesenstadt — das Gewirr der Stollen, Tunnel und Kanäle, der Leitungen, Rohre und Kabel in den Eingeweiden Londons, so kompliziert und sensibel wie das Innere eines Menschen! Jedesmal, wenn ein Londoner an einem Hahn dreht, auf einen Schalter drückt, ein Ei kocht, ein Bad benützt, telephoniert oder eine Fahrt unternimmt, sollte er sich sagen: „Was hier geschieht, ist ein Wunder." Man möchte meinen, wenn man ein so heikles Gewirk an irgendeinem Punkt antastete, müßte das Ganze zusammenbrechen. Aber wie wir im letzten Krieg gesehen haben, erweist es sich — in guten und zuverlässigen Händen — als von magischer Dauerhaftigkeit.

Am liebsten ist mir zweifellos der Fluß, und das ist nicht nur eine persönliche Eigenheit. Ohne den Fluß hätte es London nie gegeben, und ohne ihn könnte es heute nicht existieren. Er ist Londons Vorratskammer, sein Brunnen, sein Licht und seine Wärme — seine Geschichte. Er sollte jedem lieb und teuer sein.

In unserer schönen Bildergalerie überwiegt natürlich das Londoner „Festland". Aber auch hier zeigt sich die Vielfalt des Stroms: die prächtige Tower Bridge, der alte Tower (der es irgendwie fertigbringt, immer wie ein neues Spielzug auszusehen) und darunter Cockney-Kinder beim Spiel im Sand (wußten Sie, daß auf Anregung des großen Londoners „Tubby" Clayton all dieser Sand 1934 liebevoll auf dem Wasser herangebracht wurde, damit das Ostend seinen eigenen Strand habe?); St. Paul's Cathedral; jener herrliche Blick von Blackfriars Bridge mit den fröhlichen kleinen Sommerwolken; beladene Leichter, die an den Bojen liegen; Somerset House im Flutlicht, das Parlament, der Clock Tower, die Sphinx, die County Hall, die Katze auf der Schiffswerft, die Tate Gallery — und das Standbild von Samuel Plimsoll, das nur wenige kennen.

Wer noch nie mit forschenden, aufmerksamen Blicken durch London gewandert ist, der wird es jetzt tun.

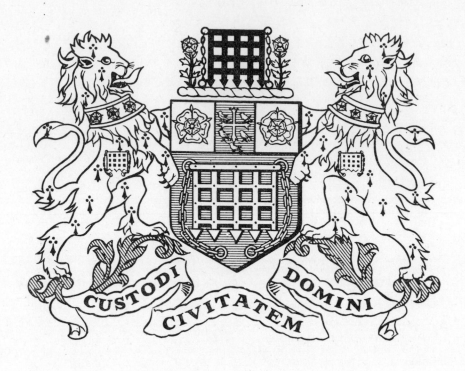

CUSTODI DOMINI CIVITATEM

THE ARMS OF THE CITY OF WESTMINSTER
LES ARMES DE LA CITÉ DE WESTMINSTER
WAPPEN DER CITY WESTMINSTER

Index

COLOUR PLATES

Piccadilly Circus

Petticoat Lane

Londres a un Passé

LONDON HAS A PAST

Londons Vergangenheit

Cleopatra's Needle, Victoria Embankment. Brought from Alexandria in 1878, it originally stood at Heliopolis

L'Aiguille de Cléopâtre, Victoria Embankment. Rapportée d'Alexandrie en 1878, elle s'élevait à l'origine à Héliopolis

Nadel der Cleopatra, Victoria-Kai. 1878 aus Alexandria nach London gekommen, ursprünglich in Heliopolis

The Griffin, marking the site of the old Temple Bar, one of the gates of old London
Le Griffon, qui marque l'emplacement de l'ancien Temple Bar, l'une des portes de Londres
Der Griffin, Kennzeichen des einstigen Standorts der Temple Bar, eines Zufahrtstors zur Londoner Innenstadt

19

The Cloisters, Lincoln's Inn, beneath the chapel erected from the design of Inigo Jones in 1620
Le péristyle de Lincoln's Inn, sous la chapelle édifiée d'après les plans d'Inigo Jones en 1620
Kreuzgang, Lincoln's Inn, am Fuß der Kapelle, die 1620 nach den Plänen von Inigo Jones errichtet wurde

Middle Gate, Tower of London, the most famous fortress in Great Britain, and once the most infamous prison
Middle Gate, à la Tour de Londres, la plus célèbre forteresse de Grande-Bretagne, qui fut aussi une prison de triste mémoire
Mitteltor des Tower, der berühmtesten Festung Londons und des einstmals berüchtigtsten Gefängnisses

Dragon with cannon, Horse Guards Parade. It commemorates the raising of the siege of Cadiz by Wellington
Le Dragon au canon, Horse Guards Parade, commémore la levée du siège de Cadix par Wellington
Lindwurm mit Geschütz, Horse Guards Parade, zur Erinnerung an die Aufhebung der Belagerung von Cadiz durch Wellington

Old cannon, Tower of London
Vieux canon à la Tour de Londres
Altes Geschütz, Tower

23

Southwark Cathedral, by London Bridge, a fine Gothic church which was founded in the 12th century
Southwark Cathedral (London Bridge), belle église gothique du XIIème siècle
Southwark Cathedral an der London Bridge, eine schöne gotische Kirche aus dem 12. Jahrhundert

John Pinches, Albert Embankment, medal and shield makers, a curious contrast to its modern neighbours
L'atelier de John Pinches, Albert Embankment, fabricant d'écussons et médailles, entouré d'immeubles modernes
John Pinches am Albert-Kai, Schilder- und Medaillenwerkstatt, ein seltsamer Gegensatz zu den modernen Nachbargebäuden

Romney's House, Hampstead, where George Romney, the 18th-century painter, lived and worked
Romney's House, à Hampstead. La maison et l'atelier de George Romney, peintre du XVIIIème siècle
Romney's House, Hampstead, wo George Romney, ein Maler des 18. Jahrhunderts, lebte und arbeitete

The Old Curiosity Shop, off Kingsway, immortalised by Charles Dickens in his novel
The Old Curiosity Shop, près de Kingsway, immortalisée par Charles Dickens
Old Curiosity Shop in einer Nebenstraße von Kingsway, von Charles Dickens in seinem Werk „Der Raritätenladen" verewigt

Old sign on the building of the Company of Stationers, a guild of printers and booksellers founded in 1556

Vieille enseigne sur l'immeuble de la Compagnie des papetiers, corporation des imprimeurs et libraires fondée en 1556

Altes Wahrzeichen auf dem Gebäude der Company of Stationers, einer 1556 gegründeten Zunft der Drucker und Buchhändler

Grove Lodge, Hampstead, once the home of John Galsworthy, the novelist and playwright
Grove Lodge, Hampstead, où vécut naguère le romancier et auteur dramatique John Galsworthy
Grove Lodge, Hampstead, einst der Wohnsitz des Romanschriftstellers und Dramatikers John Galsworthy

29

Charing Cross marks the last of thirteen resting-places of Queen Eleanor on her burial journey to Westminster

Charing Cross, la dernière des treize stations de la dépouille mortelle de la reine Eléonore avant son inhumation à Westminster

Charing Cross, die letzte der dreizehn Stationen, an denen der Leichenzug von Königin Eleanor auf seinem Weg nach Westminster hielt

Londres possède des Traditions

LONDON HAS
TRADITIONS

Londons Traditionen

31

Buckingham Palace, the London residence of the Royal Family
Buckingham Palace, résidence londonienne de la famille royale
Buckingham Palace, die Londoner Residenz der königlichen Familie

St James's Palace, which until 1837 was the official residence of the sovereigns of England
St-James's Palace, qui fut jusqu'en 1837 la résidence officielle des souverains anglais
St. James's Palace, bis 1837 die offizielle Residenz der englischen Monarchen

The Bank of England, founded in 1694 by a Scotsman
La Banque d'Angleterre, fondée en 1694 par un Écossais
Die Bank von England, 1694 von einem Schotten gegründet

The Royal Exchange, Cornhill, is actually the third Royal Exchange, the first two having been destroyed by fire
La Bourse (Royal Exchange), Cornhill, la troisième de ce nom, les deux premières ayant été détruites par l'incendie
Royal Exchange in Cornhill, die dritte Börse dieses Namens, nachdem die ersten beiden vom Feuer zerstört wurden

The 'Old Bailey', the Central Criminal Court, surmounted by the famous figure of Justice
L'Old Bailey, la Cour centrale d'Assises, dominée par la fameuse allégorie de la Justice
Strafgerichtshof Old Bailey, überragt von der berühmten Figur der Justitia

Somerset House, which contains a complete record of all births, marriages and deaths in England since 1838
Somerset House, contenant les archives complètes des naissances, mariages et décès enregistrés en Angleterre depuis 1838
Somerset House, wo ein komplettes Register aller Geburten, Trauungen und Todesfälle seit 1838 in England aufbewahrt wird

The Royal Naval College, Greenwich, designed by Wren, is today the training school of officers of the Royal Navy
Cet édifice construit par Wren à Greenwich est aujourd'hui l'école des officiers de la Marine Royale
Das Royal Naval College in Greenwich, von Christopher Wren entworfen, heute eine Schule für Offiziere der Royal Navy

Headquarters, Duke of York's Regiment, Chelsea
Quartier général du Regiment du duc d'York à Chelsea
Hauptquartier, Regiment des Herzogs von York, Chelsea

The Law Courts in the Strand, built between 1874 and 1882, contain twenty-three courts and 1,100 rooms
Les Law Courts, Strand, construites entre 1874 et 1882, ne comptent pas moins de 23 salles d'audience et 1,100 pièces
Die Gerichtsgebäude am „Strand", 1874–1882 erbaut, umfassen 23 Gerichte und 1100 Räume

Guildhall, where a new Lord Mayor is elected annually
Guildhall, où le Lord Maire de Londres est élu chaque année
Das Rathaus: dort wird jährlich der neue Oberbürgermeister gewählt

Westminster Abbey, where the English sovereigns from Edward the Confessor onwards have been crowned

L'Abbaye de Westminster, où ont été couronnés les souverains anglais depuis Édouard le Confesseur

Westminster Abbey, die Krönungsstätte der englischen Monarchen seit Eduard dem Bekenner

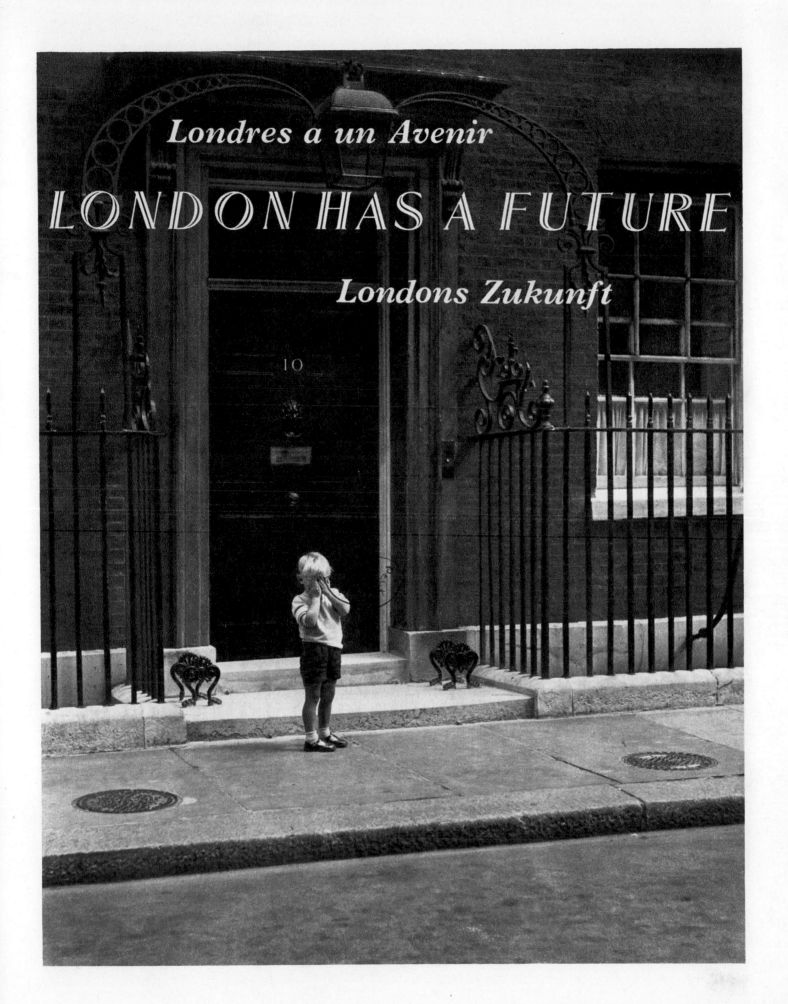

Londres a un Avenir

LONDON HAS A FUTURE

Londons Zukunft

New design in commercial buildings: offices over the Bank of Scotland, Knightsbridge
Bureaux modernes au dessus d'une succursale de la Banque d'Écosse, Knightsbridge
Ein neuer Stil der Geschäftshäuser: Büros über der Bank von Schottland, Knightsbridge

Modern office block in Sloane Street, Chelsea
Immeuble à usage de bureaux dans Sloane Street, Chelsea
Moderner Büroblock in der Sloane Street, Chelsea

New religious architecture: a modern church tower in Pont Street, Chelsea
Architecture religieuse contemporaine: Église de Pont Street, Chelsea
Neue religiöse Architektur: moderner Kirchturm in der Pont Street, Chelsea

St George's Cathedral, Southwark, rebuilt in 1958
La cathédrale St-Georges à Southwark, reconstruite en 1958
St. George's Cathedral, Southwark, 1958 wiederaufgebaut

47

New building on war-damaged site, London Wall
Nouvel immeuble sur l'emplacement d'un quartier détruit par les bombardements, London Wall
Neues Gebäude auf einem Trümmergelände aus dem Krieg, London Wall

Out of the ruins: Bunhill Row, Borough of Finsbury
Une autre reconstruction d'après-guerre: Bunhill Row, dans le bourg de Finsbury
Aus den Ruinen: Bunhill Row, Stadtbezirk Finsbury

Albert Embankment from the river; the tiny building in the gap is John Pinches (page 25), which has since been demolished
L'Albert Embankment, vu du fleuve. La petite maison que l'on aperçoit est l'atelier de John Pinches (page 25), récemment detruite
Albert-Kai, vom Fluß aus gesehen; das winzige Bauwerk in dem Durchblick ist die Werkstatt von John Pinches (Seite 25)

The Royal Festival Hall, built in 1951, and the old Shot Tower, once used for making gunshot
Le Royal Festival Hall, bâti en 1951, et la vieille Shot Tower, ancienne fabrique de boulets
Die 1951 erbaute Royal Festival Hall, daneben der alte Shot Tower, wo einst Munition hergestellt wurde

51

London University
L'Université de Londres
Die Londoner Universität

52

The London Planetarium, a 'Theatre of the Skies' adjoining Madame Tussaud's waxworks museum in Marylebone Road
Le London Planétarium, «théâtre des cieux», tout proche du fameux musée de cires de Madame Tussaud, dans Marylebone Road
Das Londoner Planetarium grenzt an Madame Tussauds Wachsfigurenkabinett in der Marylebone Road

St Paul's Church, Portman Square, and modern building adjacent
L'Église St-Paul, Portman Square, entourée d'édifices modernes
St. Paul's Church, Portman Square, und angrenzendes modernes Gebäude

Looking across Southwark Bridge: on the right, three modern office blocks
Vue prise de Southwark Bridge: à droite, trois immeubles commerciaux modernes
Blick über die Southwark Bridge: rechts drei moderne Büroblocks

'Prospero and Ariel', sculpture by Eric Gill over the entrance to Broadcasting House

«Prospero et Ariel», sculpture d'Eric Gill à l'entrée de Broadcasting House

„Prospero und Ariel", eine Skulptur von Eric Gill über dem Tor von Broadcasting House

Londres possède des Bâtiments

LONDON HAS BUILDINGS

Londons Bauwerke

Piccadilly Circus and the Quadrant. Regent Street, built to the designs of John Nash in 1816 and re-built between 1923 and 1927
Piccadilly Circus et le Quadrant de Regent Street, édifié par John Nash en 1816 et reconstruit entre 1923 et 1927
Piccadilly Circus und Quadrant, Regent Street, 1816 erbaut nach einem Entwurf von John Nash, 1923–1927 wiedererrichtet

58

St Paul's Cathedral, designed by Wren just after the Great Fire of 1666, still dominates London's skyline
La cathédrale St-Paul, bâtie par Wren tout de suite après le Grand Incendie de 1666, domine encore la ville
St. Paul's Cathedral, entworfen von Wren nach dem Großen Feuer des Jahres 1666, beherrscht die Silhouette von London

The Tower of Westminster Cathedral, Victoria. The cathedral, in the early Byzantine style, was completed in 1903

La tour de la cathédrale de Westminster, Victoria, dans le style byzantin primitif, a été achevée en 1903

Der Turm der Westminster Cathedral, Victoria, im frühbyzantinischen Stil erbaut, 1903 fertiggestellt

St Mary-le-Strand Church

L'Église St-Mary-le-Strand

Die Kirche St. Mary-le-Strand

Admiralty Arch, a memorial to Queen Victoria, as seen from the Mall
L'arche de l'Amirauté, dédiée à la mémoire de la reine Victoria, vue du Mall
Der Admiralty Arch zum Gedächtnis von Königin Victoria, vom Mall aus gesehen

Carlton House Terrace along the Mall, a fine example of late Regency architecture, was completed about 1831
Carlton House Terrace, sur le Mall, bel exemple de l'architecture de la fin de la Régence, fut achevée en 1831
Carlton House Terrace am Mall, ein schönes Beispiel der späten Regency-Bauweise, 1831 fertiggestellt

The Tate Gallery, Millbank, contains one of the finest collections of modern art
La Tate Gallery, Millbank, contient l'une des plus belles collections nationales d'art moderne
Die Tate Gallery, Millbank, enthält eine der schönsten nationalen Sammlungen moderner Kunst

Port of London Authority administrative building, Tower Hill, opened in 1922

Le siège de l'Administration du Port de Londres, Tower Hill, ouvert en 1922

Verwaltungsgebäude der Port of London Authority, Tower Hill, 1922 eröffnet

The inner courtyard of the Temple, dating from the 12th century, now part of the Inns of Court
La cour du Temple date de XIIème siècle. Elle fait maintenant partie des Inns of Court
Innenhof des ehemaligen Temple, aus dem 12. Jahrhundert, heute ein Bestandteil der Gerichtsgebäude

Staple Inn, High Holborn, once a hostelry of the wool trade, is now used for offices
Staple Inn, High Holborn, ancienne auberge des marchands de laine, est aujourd'hui occupée par des bureaux
Staple Inn, High Holborn, einstmals eine Herberge der Wollkaufleute, heute als Bürogebäude benutzt

The Tower of the Imperial Institute, Kensington, a famous landmark. The building is mainly occupied by London University
La tour de l'Institut impérial, Kensington. L'édifice est occupé en grande partie par l'Université de Londres
Der Turm des Imperial Institute, Kensington. Das Gebäude wird hauptsächlich von der Londoner Universität in Anspruch genommen

Lincoln's Inn, Chancery Lane, which far from being an 'inn' is part of the institution which qualifies lawyers
Lincoln's Inn, Chancery Lane, n'est pas une auberge, mais le lieu où sont formés les futurs avocats
Lincoln's Inn, Sitz einer Vereinigung von Rechtsanwälten, deren Mitglieder berechtigt sind, vor Gericht zu plädieren

The Royal Albert Hall, Kensington, shaped like a Roman arena, was opened in 1871
Le Royal Albert Hall, Kensington, en forme d'arènes romaines, a été inauguré en 1871
Die Royal Albert Hall, Kensington, in der Form einer römischen Arena, 1871 eröffnet

The British Museum, one of the world's greatest museums, housing a vast collection of Egyptian, Greek and Roman antiquities
Le British Museum, l'un des plus grands musées, abrite une riche collection d'antiquités égyptiennes et gréco-romaines
Das Britische Museum birgt reiche Sammlungen ägyptischer, griechischer und römischer Altertümer

The Admiralty, the administrative centre of the Royal Navy. Radio contact with the Fleet is maintained from here
L'Amirauté est le Ministère de la Marine. Le contact y est maintenu en permanence par radio avec les unités de la Flotte
Die Admiralität, Verwaltungszentrum der Royal Navy, das mit der Flotte in Funkverbindung steht

Londres a des Monuments

LONDON HAS
MONUMENTS

Londons Denkmäler

The Duke of York's Column, the Mall, erected to the memory of Frederick, second son of George III
La Duke of York's Column, sur le Mall, érigée à la mémoire de Frederick, second fils de George III
Säule des Herzogs von York am Mall, errichtet zum Andenken an Frederick, den zweiten Sohn Georgs III.

Nelson's Column, Trafalgar Square, the well-known memorial to Admiral Horatio Nelson
Nelson's Column à Trafalgar Square, célèbre monument à la mémoire de l'amiral Horatio Nelson
Die Nelson-Säule, Trafalgar Square, das bekannte Denkmal für Admiral Horatio Nelson

The Albert Memorial stands close to the Royal Albert Hall and serves as an impressive monument to a popular Consort
L'Albert Memorial proche du Royal Albert Hall, impressionnant monument dédié à la mémoire d'un consort très aimé
Albert Memorial, nahe der Royal Albert Hall, ein eindrucksvolles Denkmal an einen beim Volk beliebten Prinzgemahl

Pigeons roosting on the statue of King George IV, Trafalgar Square
Pigeons perchés sur la statue du roi George IV à Trafalgar Square
Tauben bei der Rast auf dem Standbild König Georgs IV., Trafalgar Square

The Peter Pan statue, Kensington Gardens, an interpretation by Sir George Frampton of the character created by James Barrie
Le statue de Peter Pan à Kensington Gardens, personnification par Sir George Frampton du fameux personnage de James Barrie
Standbild des Peter Pan, der berühmter, von James Barrie ins Leben gerufenen Gestalt, in Kensington Gardens

Known as 'Achilles', this statue to the Duke of Wellington in Hyde Park was erected in 1822 by the women of England
«Achille», statue dédiée au duc de Wellington, à Hyde Park, a été érigée en 1822 par les femmes d'Angleterre
Das Standbild „Achilles", zum Andenken an den Herzog von Wellington 1822 im Hyde Park von den Frauen Englands errichtet

Statue of Captain R. F. Scott, the Antarctic explorer, made by Lady Scott and erected in 1912 at Wellington Place
La statue du capitaine R. F. Scott, explorateur de l'Antarctique, due à Lady Scott, a été érigée en 1912 à Wellington Place
Standbild des Antarktisforschers Captain R. F. Scott, von Lady Scott geschaffen und 1912 am Wellington Place errichtet

The Samuel Plimsoll Memorial, Embankment. Plimsoll, throughout his life, sought reform of the laws governing shipping
Samuel Plimsoll Memorial, Embankment. Plimsoll a consacrée sa vie à la réforme des lois sur le chargement des navires
Samuel Plimsoll Memorial am Kai. Plimsoll kämpfte sein Leben lang für Reformen im Seerecht

The Royal Artillery Memorial, Hyde Park Corner, and the Quadriga, representing Peace alighting on the Chariot of War
Le Royal Artillery Memorial, Hyde Park Corner, et le Quadrige, qui représente la Paix se posant sur le chariot de la Guerre
Royal Artillery Memorial, Hyde Park Corner, und die Quadriga, eine Darstellung des Friedens, wie er den Kriegswagen besteigt

The Victoria Memorial in the Mall depicts Queen Victoria among symbolic figures of Justice, Truth, Courage and Constancy
Le Victoria Memorial, dans le Mall, évoque les allégories de la Justice, de la Vérité, du Courage et de la Constance
Das Victoria Memorial am Mall zeigt die symbolischen Gestalten der Gerechtigkeit, der Wahrheit, des Mutes und der Beständigkeit

The George VI Statue, the Mall

La statue de George VI, le Mall

Standbild König Georgs VI., Mall

84

The Royal Air Force Memorial,
Victoria Embankment

Le Royal Air Force Memorial,
Victoria Embankment

Royal Air Force Memorial,
Victoria-Kai

85

Statue to the Cavalry of the Empire, Stanhope Gate, Hyde Park, representing St George and the Dragon
Statue dédiée à la Cavalerie de l'Empire, Stanhope Gate, Hyde Park, représentant St-George et le Dragon
Standbild für die Cavalry of the Empire, Stanhope Gate, Hyde Park, eine Darstellung St. Georgs mit dem Drachen

Londres peut séduire

LONDON HAS LOVELINESS

Londons Liebreiz

Only twenty minutes from the centre of London: Squire's Mount Croft, a quiet street of cottages in Hampstead
A vingt minutes seulement du centre de Londres: Squire's Mount Croft, rue de calmes et coquettes maisons à Hampstead
Nur zwanzig Minuten vom Zentrum Londons entfernt: Squire's Mount Croft, eine friedliche Reihe kleiner Häuschen in Hampstead

The Convent and entrance to St Alban's Church, Holborn
Le Couvent et l'entrée de l'église St-Alban, Holborn
Konvent und Eingang zur St. Alban's Church, Holborn

Wrought iron gates, Queen Mary's Gardens, Regent's Park
Grilles de fer forgé, Queen Mary's Gardens, Regent's Park
Schmiedeeiserne Tore, Queen Mary's Gardens, Regent's Park

Wrought iron gates, Lincoln's Inn
Grilles de fer forgé, Lincoln's Inn
Schmiedeeiserne Tore, Lincoln's Inn

'The Grenadier' in Wilton Row, Knightsbridge, said to be the smallest 'pub' in London
«The Grenadier», Wilton Row, Knightsbridge, serait, dit-on, la plus petite auberge de Londres
„Der Grenadier" in Wilton Row, Knightsbridge, angeblich das kleinste Wirtshaus von London

A moment away from the city's hustle: the gardens at Kensington Palace
Quelques instants de répit: les jardins de Kensington Palace
Einen Augenblick fern vom Getriebe der Stadt: die Gärten von Kensington Palace

Water contains every shape: fountains in Kensington Gardens
Fontaines à Kensington Gardens
Springbrunnen in Kensington Gardens

94

A fountain of mermaids at Regent's Park
Fontaine de sirènes à Regent's Park
Nixen-Brunnen in Regent's Park

'The Wrestlers' by Rodin, Embankment Gardens
«Les lutteurs», oeuvre de Rodin aux Embankment Gardens
„Die Ringkämpfer" von Rodin, Embankment Gardens

Soho Square, in the heart of the most congested area of London
Soho Square, au cœur de l'un des quartiers les plus encombrés de la capitale
Soho Square, im Herzen des übervölkertsten Stadtteils von London

Shadows cast by the sun: Hampstead Heath
Jeux d'ombres et de lumière: Hampstead Heath
Licht und Schatten: Hampstead Heath

And by the moon: looking west from Southwark Bridge
Au clair de la lune: vue prise de Southwark Bridge en direction de l'ouest
Im Mondschein: Blick von der Southwark Bridge nach Westen

Big Ben illuminated, as seen from Parliament Square
Big Ben illuminé, vu de Parliament Square
Big Ben illuminiert, vom Parliament Square aus gesehen

Illuminated fountains in Trafalgar Square, in front of St Martin's-in-the-Fields
Fontaines illuminées à Trafalgar Square, en face de l'église St-Martin's-in-the-Fields
Illuminierte Springbrunnen auf dem Trafalgar Square, vor der Kirche St. Martin's-in-the-Fields

A view from the bridge: Queen Mary's Gardens, Regent's Park
Vue du pont: Queen Mary's Gardens, Regent's Park
Ein Blick von der Brücke: Queen Mary's Gardens, Regent's Park

Londres possède un Fleuve   *Londons Fluss*

LONDON HAS A RIVER

Spanning the river: Westminster Bridge, leading to the Houses of Parliament
Enjambant le fleuve: Westminster Bridge, par lequel on accède au Parlement
Quer über den Fluß zu den Parlamentsgebäuden: Westminster Bridge

On Westminster Bridge: St Thomas's Hospital, and further up a glimpse of the new buildings along the Albert Embankment
De Westminster Bridge: vue sur St-Thomas's Hospital et les nouveaux immeubles de l'Albert Embankment
Auf der Westminster Bridge: St. Thomas's Hospital, weiter unten die neuen Gebäude am Albert-Kai

Speed-boats on the Thames as seen from Blackfriars Bridge
Vedettes sur la Tamise, à hauteur de Blackfriars Bridge
Schnellboote auf der Themse, von der Blackfriars Bridge aus gesehen

Flocking together: swans and houseboats on Chelsea Embankment
Naviguant ensemble: cygnes et péniches sur le fleuve, Chelsea Embankment
Friedlich vereint: Schwäne und Hausboote am Chelsea-Kai

River ferries in front of County Hall, the headquarters of the London County Council
Bateaux de promenade en face de County Hall, siège du Conseil du Comté de Londres
Flußfähren vor der County Hall, dem Sitz des Londoner Grafschaftsrats

Swans and onlookers along the Thames, Blackfriars
Cygnes et spectateurs sur le fleuve, Blackfriars
Schwäne und Zuschauer an der Themse, Blackfriars

The 'Wellington', Embankment, a sloop of the Royal Navy, now the headquarters of the Royal Company of Master Mariners
Le «Wellington» (Embankment), aviso de la Marine royale, siège administratif de la Compagnie royale des maîtres mariniers
Die „Wellington" am Kai, ein Schiff der Royal Navy, jetzt Standort der Royal Company of Master Mariners

Tower Bridge, close to the Tower of London, can raise its central bascules to allow the passage of large ships
Tower Bridge, près de la Tour de Londres, peut se lever dans sa partie centrale pour laisser passage aux gros navires
Die Tower Bridge kann ihre mittleren Zugbrücken hochgehen lassen, um großen Schiffen die Durchfahrt zu ermöglichen

Lambeth Pier and Lambeth Palace, the residence of the Archbishop of Canterbury
Lambeth Pier et Lambeth Palace, résidence des archevêques de Cantorbéry
Lambeth Pier und Lambeth Palace, Sitz des Erzbischofs von Canterbury

The 'Cutty Sark', permanently preserved at Greenwich, was the fastest of the 19th-century tea clippers
Le «Cutty Sark», le plus rapide des clippers qui transportaient le thé d'Orient au XIXème siècle, est conservé à Greenwich
Die „Cutty Sark", in Greenwich für immer vor Anker gegangen, war einer der schnellsten Segler des 19. Jahrhunderts

The 'Discovery', Embankment, the ship in which Captain Scott made his expedition to the South Pole
«Le Discovery» (Embankment), navire à bord duquel le capitaine Scott explora le pôle sud
Die „Discovery" am Kai, das Schiff, auf dem Captain Scott zu seiner Südpolexpedition ausfuhr

Living on the river: dockyard cat, Queenhithe

Habitant des rives: chat de chantier, Queenhithe

Ein Leben, das der Fluß beherrscht: Katze auf der Schiffswerft, Queenhithe

Londres a du Travail à faire

LONDON HAS WORK TO DO

Londons Arbeit

It's all a matter of balance: Covent Garden fruit and vegetable market
C'est uniquement une question d'équilibre: le marché des fruits et légumes à Covent Garden
Alles nur eine Frage des Gleichgewichts: Obst- und Gemüsemarkt in Covent Garden

Keeping the pot boiling: pitch burner on a new building site, Moorgate
Chaud, chaud! Goudronneur sur un chantier à Moorgate
Der Kessel darf nicht kalt werden: Teerbrenner auf der Baustelle, Moorgate

Ice merchant at Billingsgate fish market
Marchand de glace sur le marché aux poissons à Billingsgate
Eisverkäufer auf dem Fischmarkt von Billingsgate

Keeping an eye on the road: street
cleaner, Strand

Chargé de la toilette des rues:
cantonnier sur le Strand

Mit Gründlichkeit und Sorgfalt:
Straßenkehrer, Strand

120

Carrying the good news: sandwich-
man outside the Royal Academy,
Piccadilly

Porteur de bonnes nouvelles: un
homme-sandwich devant le Royal
Academy, Piccadilly

Erfreuliche Neuigkeiten: Sandwich-
mann vor der Royal Academy,
Piccadilly

Maintenance of the roads: road-mender, Upper Thames Street, with Cannon Street Station in the background
Entretien des routes: travaux à Upper Thames Street. Au loin, le gare de Cannon Street
Alles braucht seine Pflege: Straßenarbeiter, Upper Thames Street. Im Hintergrund der Bahnhof Cannon Street

Maintenance of London's lights, Trafalgar Square
Entretien des lampadaires, Trafalgar Square
Londons Lichtermeer muß aufrechterhalten werden: Trafalgar Square

Hand-drawn: barrow-boy at Hyde Park Corner
Marchand des quatre saisons à Hyde Park Corner
Handbetrieb: Straßenhändler mit Karren, Hyde Park Corner

Horse-drawn: door-to-door greengrocer, Upper Cheyne Row, Chelsea
Marchand de légumes en tournée, Upper Cheyne Row, Chelsea
Mit 1 PS: Fahrender Gemüsehändler, Upper Cheyne Row, Chelsea

125

Unloading timber from a Thames barge
Déchargement de bois sur les rives de la Tamise
Themse-Leichter beim Löschen von Holz

Everyone has gone back to work: Hyde Park after the lunch-hour crowds
Chacun est retourné au travail: Hyde Park après les heures de midi
Alles ist wieder an die Arbeit gegangen: der Hyde Park nach der Essenszeit

Workmen cleaning a statue, Trafalgar Square
Nettoyage d'une statue, Trafalgar Square
Arbeiter bei der Reinigung eines Standbilds, Trafalgar Square

Londres a des Moments de Loisir

LONDON HAS
TIME · OFF

Londons Freizeit

Swingboats, Jack Bond's Fair, Hampstead Heath
Balançoires, Jack Bond's Fair, Hampstead Heath
Schiffsschaukeln, Jack Bond's Fair, Hampstead Heath

Artists playing chess at the 'Open-air Gallery', Knightsbridge
Une partie d'échecs entre artistes, «Open-air Gallery», Knightsbridge
Künstler beim Schachspiel in der „Freiluft-Galerie", Knightsbridge

Young fishermen, The Serpentine, Hyde Park
Jeunes pêcheurs, la Serpentine, Hyde Park
Junge Fischer, Serpentine, Hyde Park

Tower Beach

Even younger fishermen, Vale of Health, Hampstead Heath
Plus jeunes encore . . . Vale of Health, Hampstead Heath
Noch jüngere Fischer, Vale of Health, Hampstead

Round Pond

Exploring a hollow tree in Hyde Park
Exploration d'un tronc creux, Hyde Park
Ein hohler Baum im Hyde Park wird erforscht

Children paddling in Whitestone Pond, Hampstead
Jeux d'enfants à Whitestone Pond, Hampstead
Kinder beim Plantschen im Whitestone Pond, Hampstead

Proms queue, Royal Albert Hall
Une queue à l'entrée du Royal Albert Hall, où se donnent les Promenade Concerts
Alles wartet auf das Promenadenkonzert, Royal Albert Hall

On the riverside near the Tower
Sur les bords de la Tamise, près de la Tour de Londres
Am Fluß in der Nähe des Tower

Indoor pleasures: the 'Prospect of Whitby', Wapping, one of the oldest inns in London
Plaisir de la conversation: le «Prospect of Whitby», Wapping, l'un des plus anciens pubs de Londres
Stammtischfreuden: der „Prospect of Whitby", Wapping, eines der ältesten Wirtshäuser von London

138

A corner of 'Dirty Dick's', Bishopsgate, named after its unkempt owner in the 18th century

Un coin du «Dirty Dick's», Bishopsgate, qui doit son nom à un propriétaire un peu . . . négligé qu'il eut au XVIIIème siècle

Ein Stückchen „Dirty Dick's", Bishopsgate, benannt nach dem ungepflegten Besitzer im 18. Jahrhundert

139

The Old Vic, Waterloo Road, a theatre where mainly Shakespeare's plays are performed
L'Old Vic, Waterloo Road, où l'on joue le plus souvent Shakespeare
Old Vic, Waterloo Road, ein Theater, in dem hauptsächlich Stücke von Shakespeare aufgeführt werden

Sailing a model yacht, the Round Pond, Kensington Gardens
Bateaux à voiles, Round Pond, Kensington Gardens
Fahrt einer Modelljacht, Round Pond, Kensington Gardens

'Playing guns' outside the Admiralty
Un futur artilleur, devant le bâtiment de l'Amirauté
„Kanone schußbereit!" – Vor der Admiralität

Men at play: football match at Chelsea Royal Hospital sports ground
Jeux: un match de football sur le terrain du Chelsea Royal Hospital
Männer beim Spiel: Fußballkampf auf dem Sportgelände des Chelsea Royal Hospital

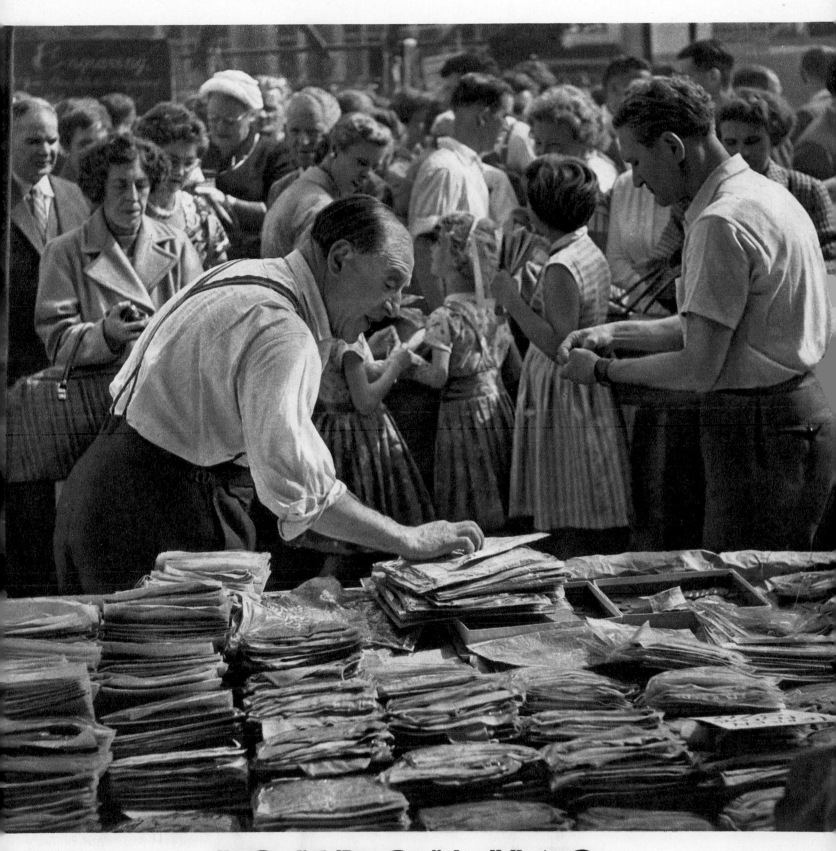

LONDON HAS
LONDONERS

Protest meeting, Trafalgar Square
Meeting de protestation, Trafalgar Square
Protestversammlung, Trafalgar Square

Protest Meeting, Speakers' Corner, Hyde Park
Meeting de protestation à Speakers' Corner, Hyde Park
Protestversammlung, Speakers' Corner, Hyde Park

147

Alone: Blackfriars
Seul: à Blackfriars
Allein: Blackfriars

Together: Knightsbridge
Ensemble: à Knightsbridge
Zu zweit: Knightsbridge

149

On duty: night guard approaching the Bank of England
En service: le garde de nuit s'approchant de la Banque d'Angleterre
Im Dienst: Wachmannschaft für die Nacht auf dem Weg zur Bank von England

Off duty: schoolgirls on Hampstead Heath
En congé: écolières en promenade à Hampstead Heath
Dienstfrei: Schulmädchen auf Hampstead Heath

Coffee for one: prom-goer, Royal Albert Hall
Un bon café: un habitué des «Promenade Concerts», Royal Albert Hall
Kaffee für den Einzelnen Besucher des Promenadenkonzerts, Royal Albert Hall

Music for all: street musicians, Petticoat Lane
Musique populaire: un groupe de musiciens ambulants, Petticoat Lane
Musik für alle: Straßenmusikanten, Petticoat Lane

153

'This one?' Open-air Gallery, Knightsbridge
«Celui-ci?» Open-air Gallery à Knightsbridge
„Das da?" Freiluft-Galerie, Knightsbridge

'Certainly not *that* one!' Portobello Road
«Certainement pas ça!» Portobello Road
„Nein, *das* ganz bestimmt nicht!" Portobello Road

'Look, over there!' Motorcycle police, Marble Arch
«Regardez là-bas!» Officiers de police motorisé, Marble Arch
„Schau, da drüben . . ." Motorisierte Polizei, Marble Arch

'No, I mean over *there!*' Bond Street
«Non, là-bas!» Bond Street
„Nein, ich meine *dort* drüben!" Bond Street

In a hurry: office workers' lunch-hour, Fleet Street
Pressés: employés de bureau à l'heure du déjeuner, Fleet Street
In Eile: Essenspause der Büroangestellten, Fleet Street

At leisure: window-shoppers, Burlington Arcade
En léchant les vitrines . . . Flâneurs à Burlington Arcade
In aller Ruhe: Schaufensterbummel, Burlington Arcade

Oh well . . .
Et voilà . . .
Endlich . . .

160